WEAR A WOLD HAT

Memoirs of a Yorkshire Rascal

by
Fred Marwood

as retold to
Alex Marwood

Illustrated by
Michael Brookes

HUTTON PRESS

1991

Published by the Hutton Press Ltd.
130 Canada Drive, Cherry Burton, Beverley
East Yorkshire HU17 7SB

Printed by
Clifford Ward & Co. (Bridlington) Ltd.
55 West Street, Bridlington, East Yorkshire
YO15 3DZ

ISBN 1 872167 14 4

CONTENTS

6

FOREWORD

I first met Fred Marwood on September 24 1984 while visiting Birmingham, I was staying with my in-laws and my wife had embarked on her family history after helping me through several difficult stages of research into my own. One of her family she was talking to suggested we check in the Birmingham phone directory for Marwoods — and there was Fred, in a council house at Oldbury, not ten minutes' walk away from where I was staying.

I phoned and that evening we visited him, a stoutly-built man with thickset neck and shoulders and the strong, prominently-nosed features which we had come to associate with many of the Marwoods discovered in Yorkshire. You would hardly have thought he was 81 years of age, so firm was his handshake and strong his voice. And he could tell a great tale about this and that, embellished with gusto, so that over our first glass of sherry from his sideboard "cellar" I found myself shaking with laughter or enthralled with his description of his experiences since he came down from Yorkshire 50 years before and married a local girl.

After he had told me that he was born at Leavening, on the Yorkshire Wolds, in the autumn of 1903, son of John Henry Marwood, labourer, I went back home and did some checking. The Leavening family dovetailed nicely into a Yorkshire family that could be traced back clearly to the marriage of a Thomas Marwood and a Mary Tyerman at Brompton by Northallerton on October 4 1783. Excited at my discovery, I drew out his family "tree" and presented it to him when we next visited Fred. Overnight the 81-year-old retired roadworker was a man with a history, and we began a correspondence and conversations right down to the time of writing, in which he described to me many of his early memories of village life, and of what he could glean from earlier times from the recollection of others.

His descent runs as follows:

Thomas and Mary Marwood had six children, mainly at Borrowby in the North Riding parish of Leake. Of these William and George migrated south to the tiny village of Crambe, prettily

7

situated by the River Derwent near Malton. On November 25 1820 George Marwood, a farmer's servant, married Hannah Finnister and had nine children, of whom John, baptised on October 27 1861, married Elizabeth Hudson at Acklam. John Marwood became a hind — a senior farmworker who was given a cottage too on condition that he provided a female farm servant from his family. Of their six children, John Henry, baptised on December 25 1879, married Ruth Rawdin from Lincoln. They had George William, Fred, John, Doris and Ada Mary.

They say that in these parts all the Marwoods were strong Wesleyans and indeed this branch of the family had some of their children baptised at Malton Wesleyan chapel, but no entry is found for Fred, who has some direct comments to make on the matter; "The only chapel I knew was the Wesleyan in Saville Street. Goodness gracious me, Leavening was full of them. Right miserable lot, what they gave away they wouldn't ask for it back. They would skin a flint for a farthing and waste a shilling knife. I was what was known as a ranter."

The family is tangled up in official records with another clan of the same name at Leavening, I have discovered no connection between the two. Nor is there any link, at least within the last two and a half centuries, between either family and my own. However, from what I have ascertained from numerous sources it is most likely that we have a common root, for the name was restricted to a few families in the North Riding and Cleveland in Tudor times.

Whatever the case, old Fred's humorous yarns and descriptive anecdotes gave me an invaluable insight into rural life in the early years of this century, and a vivid impression of how rough and ready must have been the struggle for existence in those days before modern amenities reached the wolds.

Mind you, life must have been a bit easier if you could laugh all the way along, like Fred...

Alex Marwood,
Driffield.

Chapter One

MISCHIEF IN MUM'S CLOTHING

I was born at Leavening on October 3 1903 of very humble parents. We were a large family and times were very hard. I was one of four brothers and three sisters. My father was a farmworker and had to work long hours for very little money. Our staple diet was mainly bread and golden syrup. My mother had to do a lot of thinking to make ends meet. Like many more we had to make the best of life at the turn of the century. I wasn't very old before I realised life was not all a bed of roses.

However, regardless of the hard times my father never abused us in any way. It would be me who turned out to be the rascal of the family.

Life became very hard and the housing situation was most appalling. They must have been designed for pigsties, then changed their minds. They couldn't have been in anyone's mind as family houses; the only good thing about them was that they were stone built. They had one very small room about 10 feet by 10 feet and the back kitchen was more suitable as a rabbit hutch. There was no back door.

The standard of living was well below par. It never seemed to vary; it was the same old routine seven days a week. One good thing — the oven was close to the fire. It was never cold. When the time came to do a bit of cooking, we pulled out the half-brick that acted as a flue. We couldn't afford coal, we used to gather firewood. Timber was our main source of fuel for heating a little now and again. Even a warm oven could smell nice; it was useful to put your damp socks in at night.

Mother had to be a good schemer to make ends meet. She had to be: I can remember when my father's wage was 12 shilling a week for a 12-hour day. We had no such things as Axminster carpets. It was the bare bricks well polished with elbow grease and one home-made clip rug by the fire. It was almost the same upstairs. Just imagine what the wallpaper was like: one and a half pence (old money) a roll.

9

We had to wash with cold water. Most times in the winter it would be a lick and a promise. We had no washing machine. It all had to be done by scrubbing and the old dolly tub. The times I had to do that before I went to school!

As the family grew up the sleeping arrangements were becoming more acute due to the two bedrooms being very small and we couldn't get a full-sized bed into them. It was a case of me and my oldest brother sleeping on the floor. It was hard lines!

The clothing situation was becoming a hazard. I had to wear my brothers' cast-offs and they were almost thread-bare. I have gone to school more than once wearing my mother's cast-off black stockings with the feet cut off and sewn up, and her black buttoned boots to match, and my shirt hanging out at the back. The schoolmaster understood the situation; I wasn't the only one.

My mother did her best to feed us. We got through with a struggle. One thing I couldn't stand was the wash tub by the fire on a Saturday night. The smallest went in first in one and a half gallons of water. By the time it came to my turn the water was cold. There was no such thing as pyjamas, only a short home-made shirt.

The water situation was the worst. The brook used to run close to our house and like many more we used to go upstream a short distance to collect the drinking water as there were no such things as drains and all the slops were thrown into the brook and found their way into the river. However, we did have the water laid on. Just before the 1914-18 War you had to collect it from the street.

****

Eighty years ago children had to make their own entertainment. As youngsters we used to enjoy going to funerals and weddings. One funeral in particular was held in a very cold and windy February. The memorial service was held in the local chapel. Down came a great gust of wind and blew the coffin lid off. In trying to save it the cab-driver tripped up and his false teeth fell out. We all had a great laugh, even all the old women. The cab-driver's language was vile!

Weddings used to be fun, usually held late morning. They would get 12 pennies as hot as possible and put them on a dinner plate and the bride would throw it over the cab. It was an old wives' tale that if the plate didn't break the couple would have bad luck the rest of their life. Picking up lost pennies and spitting on your hand at the same time meant just another wedding.

Although I was a bit of a weakling — at the age of 11 I just managed to scale four stone — it didn't stop me and my pals always getting into mischief. As I got older I became known as the ringleader. I was turfed out of school three times for not singing. The schoolmaster tried to come and see the old man, but the only reply he got was that my dad had been a lad himself.

We were out in the playground one morning doing our keep-fit exercises — arms stretch and touch your toes — when all of a sudden my short trousers split from back to front. The girls behind me must have had a good laugh — but it didn't bother me, I was used to such things happening...

One morning I took a cow to a farm. I was leading it by a rope around its horns when it took off unexpectedly. There was a woman coming along on a bike. She tried to get off but, too late, and she was knocked off into the hedge, much to our amusement.

I remember the morning the fox hounds met at the bottom of the village and five of us ran off from school to follow them. We didn't get back until 4pm. What a game we had! The teacher had us all out in front of the class and tried to give us the cane — but it was all in vain. A girl who sat opposite me in class handed me a piece of paper one morning. I won't tell you what was on it but while I was busy reading it the schoolmaster had gently walked up and demanded the note. He had a shock when he read it. He had to let the matter drop on account of the girl's parents.

The schoolteacher was asking his class one day what kind of food their patents like best. Of course, Yorkshire pudding and roast beef was top of the list. Then out of the blue a bit of a dimwit put his hand up and shouted that his parents liked candles.

Asked teacher, "What gave you the idea they eat candles?"

"I was in bed and I heard my dad say, blow out the candle and let's have a bit."

We used to make our own pipes and go to the farmyard and gather dried clover. Then we would meet in a corner of the school yard. The schoolmaster looked out of his window and saw a lot of smoke going up. He caught us red-handed — but let us off with a caution. It was a lovely summer Sunday and an old tramp was asleep after being on the beer. So just for a prank my mate and I tied his feet together. What a laugh! He used every word in the dictionary. However, he freed himself after a struggle.

I had a pal next door. We were always together. We went to

chapel that Sunday afternoon for a change and sat down just below the pulpit. When the old chap got up to preach his sermon he leant forward and looked over his glasses. He didn't say anything but we had an idea what was going through his mind; "I'll bet they're a couple of rascals". His sermon was about bad lads and drunken men...

****

A mother sent her son to the shop for a small brush. The shopkeeper, being rather generous, gave the lad two brushes, and told the lad to go home and tell his mother one was sixpence and the other fivepence. When he got home he told his mother what the shopkeeper had said. She told him to go back with this message, "Tell him I will give him fivepence for the sixpence one and fourpence for the fivepence one".

The shopkeeper looked at the lad and said, "Your mother has got a nerve". The lad replied, "Yes, and it has got more 'air on than your brush 'as".

Many years ago the only means of transport to town was a horsedrawn covered cart. One Saturday morning a certain person asked the carter if he would call at a shop in town and ask the shop owner if he would send her two hams off the same pig as the last two came off.

"Yes, madam, I will deliver your message with pleasure".

The carter got to town, went into the shop and said to the manager, "Mrs so-and-so want two hams off the same pig as the last two came off".

His reply was, "When you get home tell her she can have two hams off the same pig or any other pig when she pays for the last two hams she had".

The same person went into the corner shop and told the shop keeper she had recently bought a hen and 12 day-old chickens and they had all died, and she didn't know what had gone wrong.

"Well, what did you feed them on?"

"Oh, I didn't feed them on anything. I thought they were breast-fed by the mother".

****

Shopping at the local stores was quite fun at times. Money was scarce and treacle was our main diet. I went in one morning for a penn'orth taking a cup as it was sold loose. The shopkeeper weighed the cup, got the wooden spoon — and got more on it then he expected. He was that busy trying to watch the cup and the treacle at the same time that all at once it went bang into the cup. He tried to get some out but failed. You would have thought he had lost a fortune and when I laughed he looked at me and said "Thee and thee blasted treacle!" This time at morning I had two extra slices of bread and treacle.

Many years ago Malton market place was a real shoppers' paradise. It was a case of penny wise and pound foolish. One chap used to sell crockery. He held a chamber pot up: "The first woman to put her hand up can have it for nothing".

One old woman swore she was the first, she even went so far as to say she had put two hands up. However, he gave her the pot. Then she asked him for a piece of paper.

"Sorry, not here, madam"...there was great laughter.

****

I could mention a few who were rich and unhappy, they wouldn't give you the droppings off their nose. When I was a kid at school the shopkeeper had to buy their goods in bulk and sell it to the customers at what they could afford. One was nicknamed Nip Currant — he would nip one in two to make correct weight — and another one wasn't much better — he'd break a cough lozenge in half.

One old bloke asked me to do a little job for him. He didn't say thank you, all the thanks I got was: "Some day I might find tha with the her int' gutter and might pull tha ute". He was that type of miser who would blow his nose on his hands and use as soap, and save the ash out of his pipe and use it for snuff.

Another well-known character used to go into town to the gas works with his horse and cart for coke. If it was a wet day he would give the order for the coke to be left outside until it stopped raining, as it would add a little weight to the coke (crafty!).

I learned a lot from my mother, she was a real old tearaway. If there was any trouble it was always me that had to go with her and soon the feathers would start to fly. She would never give in, if it was only an old halfpenny. There's an old saying: What's bred in the bone comes out in the flesh.

****

13

Years ago, when money was hard to come by, an old man bought a donkey and small cart. It was summertime so he went into selling greens. He was going up the street one day shouting at the top of his voice "Fresh green peas threepence a pound". He hadn't gone far when an old woman came out and said, "I'll have two pounds".

As she turned round to go back into the house she remarked to the old man, "Do you know, I haven't had a pea for six months." "Gee up, Ned" he said, "before we are washed away".

****

The working lads of my youth enjoyed some simple amusements. Once, four of us went into Scarborough for the day just for fun. We wandered up to the Spa. There was a small sideshow featuring three Zulus. It was sixpence to go in, with five standing and five sitting and a low stage. The manager, one of the three, introduced the first act: How they worship God in their native country. The second act was their heebie-jeebie dance, the devil dance and how he could dance on broken glass with his naked feet. One of them cocked his foot up for me to feel to make sure it was bare. Instead of feeling it I gave it a good old scratch and didn't he dance on one leg! He went hysterical and the manager rushed in to see what was the trouble. The Zulu did his dance but gave me a nasty look when he went off.

We then went into Gala Land and went for a ride on the Blue Lagoon. We got halfway round when the boat started to drag on the bottom. However, we got as near the end as possible and had to scramble out as best we could. All the operator could say was "It's them two fat b----s in the back of the boat".

Before the 1914-18 War Egton, eight miles inland from Whitby, used to have an annual May fair. It was later just a name except for one occasion when an old moors farmer bought a bull to sell. He was the only one there.

Some farmers having a drink had an idea for a bit of fun. One asked the landlord for a small quantity of ginger. He made it into a ball and out they went. Four of them kept the farmer talking, saying what a poor condition the bull was in. The one with the ginger wandered to the rear and put the ginger under his tail. The bull gave one bellow, tail up and off he went. It was a good job he turned right downhill to the station about half a mile away. The railway gates were shut. The speed he was going he would have made Pickering in 30 minutes.

14

The Leavening football club never really got going. You either have it or you don't, but we didn't have it, we were only locals. We had no training facilities but we did try to bring a bit of life to the drab, dreary days of winter.

Our ground was far from first-class, being very waterlogged and uneven and made for heavy going. Owing to lack of support we did not last long but we had great fun at the time.

There were no such things as showers after the match; all we had was a bowl of water, one foot at a time. We might have carried on if the younger generation had taken a bit of interest. It got where we had to bring in players from outside. Sometimes they didn't turn up and that was how the club broke up.

We once went to Slingsby where we were losing 12-0 at half-time. We finished up 35-0. It was sheer slaughter. I had to go in goal at half-time. Their centre forward was a giant of a man. There was no stopping him. I once tried to and I finished up at the back of the net with the ball.

Another time I was in goal at a home match. In those days they were allowed to charge you if you had the ball. It was getting a bit rough and the centre forward was on me all the time and I made up my mind it was him or me. So I got him. He was shaping up to head the ball in. I ran out and hit him at the back of the head with my fist. He never knew what had hit him and he never came again.

Chapter Two

SONG OF THE OLD JAM PIE

My schooldays were short-lived, I left school at the ripe old age of 12. I was given an extended holiday of eight weeks by the education committee as labour was getting very short.

Being born in the countryside could be very boring, you had to live with it to know what it was like. It was a case of what was good for your forefathers was good. enough for you, like it or not, and I soon found out how boring it could be. I went on the Monday morning to the farm where my father worked. He used to get up at 5.30 a.m. I had to fetch the horses up to get them ready for work. We used to finish about 8 o'clock at night. They were long days and I didn't need rocking to sleep. The airships used to come over to bomb York but I never heard a thing. I was paid a measly £13 for the year, live-in. The 12-hour days were long and hard and it was all go. You didn't need a coat to keep warm.

For the next three years I went to live at a farm at North Grimston. It was a case of having to. The war was getting worse and we still had to work long, hard hours. The only thing we could do all night was sit by the fire in winter or have a bit of fun with the maid. It helped to while the time away.

We used to get ten days' holiday a year in November. My wage for the first year was £24. Reckon that up in today's terms!

All those years ago, when the farming industry was in a big way and the men used to eat and sleep in the farm foreman's house. All through from Monday morning until Sunday night they got jam pie and this is the song they composed:

It was the crust of the old jam pie
That we've eaten in ages gone by
For it was young when Crippen was hung
And to eat it poor Uncle did try.
But now in the churchyard he doth lie
And he has an angel up high.

His tombstone is laid and it is made
Of the crust of the old jam pie.

Another farmer's boy song was very popular many years ago and this is how it went, very short and sweet:

All ye lads that want to get fat
Go on the wold top and wear a wold hat.
Their pies are made of iron
And bread made of bran.
It rattles in your guts
Like an old tin can.

A farmhand I knew was a little late up one morning so he took a short cut to work. It was dark and he fell down a quarry. He had to lie there until the men came to work. They saw him on the ground and went to investigate, picked him up and took him to their hut. They asked him how he felt and his reply was that he had twisted himself. He had got his trousers on back to front!

****

Working on a farm was far from pleasant. There was nothing clean about it and you never seemed to be out of a job. And what could be more frustrating than walking up and down a field all day looking at the rear end of horses, lovely scenery. It would have been much nicer if horses had been trained to walk backwards.

Winter was the worst time, when all the stock was housed up. After a hard day in the field plodding up and down it was back to the old routine, a bit of tea, then out again into the stable. More feeding and brushing down in between a bit of milking, to finish the day off.

The most awful part of the job in winter was the lighting. All we had were hurricane paraffin lamps. We scratted around in semi-darkness. I also had to help with the milking, that was one job I wasn't very fond of. The old cow would sometimes get a bit restless and lash its tail round your neck. The winter months seemed long and dreary. It was great when the spring was drawing near and to see the sun come over the horizon. The time was drawing near for the big rush.

First big job was to get on the land and prepare it for sowing the corn for the next harvest.

****

17

Martinmas was the farmworkers' holiday for ten days from the 23rd November. They were paid at one o'clock and it was the one who could get home the quickest to see mam and dad and hand over his year's earnings; it was a long time to wait. By now the great fair had assembled in the market place at Malton ready for the pickings. Marshall's were well known in the North as fairground specialists. They had come for many years.

Now just imagine, those poor chaps had been away for a year up on those Yorkshire Wolds and other places. They began to realise it was time to quench their thirst. It must have felt like being let out of jail. Myself, I had to be a spectator until after the 1914-18 War. The pubs used to shut at two and that hadn't given them time to charge their batteries, and it meant having to wait until six.

By now everything was in full swing, everyone starting to have a bit of fun. The old farmers were out looking for some cheap labour for the coming year. It was like getting butter out of a dog's throat; they would barter the men down to the last halfpenny. By late afternoon the market place was choc-a-bloc, everyone throwing their money about. In those days you could do a lot with five shillings (25p in modern money).

By the time it was six o'clock the pubs were open for the second time and it was time once more for the lads to recharge their batteries. As closing time came the fun really started. As big as they were, when it came to the time and the beer would start to talk, a lot of them were nothing but windbags shouting "Let me get at him...hold me back". There was never much blood about; it was the beer that did the talking.

By the time the second Saturday came round it was very quiet and a lot of us were ready to go back to the wild for another year.

My candid opinion as regards farm work is that it could be the most boring job going. Every job on a farm was seasonal. What could be more boring; for instance, in those days it was all horses. Whatever you were doing on the land it was the whole day looking at the rear end of the horses. You can imagine what it was like. They would be enjoying lovely fresh air and what the horses were doing at the rear, it didn't smell like ashes for roses.

****

One of the most interesting things before the war was going to farm sales. They used to bring out the horses with their tails bobbed up. The farm horseman would put a stick of moist ginger up the horse's behind. By the time he got to the selling enclosure the ginger was starting to take effect. The horse's head would be doing 150 to the minute, the other end would be doing four times that speed. The best of all was when it had to do a trot down the yard. The poor horses, up would go the rear end and a right old kick backwards, and fart like thunder. Most times there would be a repeat.

I will do my best to explain what it was like before and during the 1914 War. There were rumours going round that Kaiser Bill was preparing for war. Everyone seemed to take it with a pinch of salt, except for one man. This was Sir Mark Sykes and he was resident at the big house in Sledmere. He had other ideas; knowing full well what, if a war broke out, would be the best form of transport. this is what he did: in the summer he came round canvassing mainly for farm men who were used to horses. They formed the Wagoners' Reserve. They wouldn't require any training. Of course, there was a little reward for anyone who signed his name, and that was a lovely shining gold sovereign, very tempting.

The last time he came it wasn't long before the war broke out and the postman had to deliver the letters to the men in the fields. The biggest majority were in Bradford the same day. There was no such thing as passing a doctor's test. There was a lot of commotion and the old women still insisted the war would soon be over — a little optimistic.

Now the worst came. First was the black-out. A candle or an old paraffin lamp didn't take much blacking-out. When it was time to light up in the winter one of the family had to go out to make sure there wasn't the least glimmer of light. Not much hope of that with the oil we had to put up with. You dare not show the least sign of light, not even through the keyholes. Candle-lamps were used by the farmers, very small paraffin lamps for bicycles. Singing in the street was a serious offence.

More men were called up and the Government formed a Women's Land Army and also sent out soldiers. Many hadn't a clue about farm work. One farmer told a Land Army girl to put a lead on the cow and he would go with her to the bull and have the cow served. While the bull was doing his duty the old man remarked "I would like to do that". She replied, "Help yourself, it's your cow!"

Another farmer had one of the likely lads. When he arrived the farmer asked him if he could milk a cow. Away went the lad with the bucket. The old farmer thought he was a long time and went to investigate and there was the chap with the bucket under the cow and he had hold of the cow's tail with both hands working it up and down like a pump-handle. All the farmer could say was; "The old cow seems to be enjoying it!"

During that war in my local town (Malton), it was customary for the band to march and play the new recruits to the station for national service. Not far in front the policeman was escorting a man to the same station for a spell in jail. He looked at the policeman and remarked, "It's the first time I have been played to jail". He had done a few trips before.

Towards the end of 1916 everything was getting very scarce. You were never lucky enough to find any fag ends in the street and not much black-out of chimneys. The wives used to do a trip to the woods. It was a blessing the Sunday joint didn't take too much cooking. We had to be content with the gravy.

I spent a year working for a farmer in Leavening. We were always getting into trouble with the local constable for singing in the street. His language was vile. One night he caught us and said: "What the b--- hell do you think you are doing? Them poor soldiers are up to their knees in b--- mud and you b--- singing in the street. Next time you'll be down to the station, locked up."

But it made no difference!

****

Before the 1914-18 War the villages used to have their own annual feast days. But it was Leavening that made it two great days, always known as the Club Feast and always on the second Friday and Saturday in July. It was something we would look forward to.

By early morning the local show people would start to arrive to get the best position.

The top pub row was full of sideshows, coconut shies and swings etc. There was one old woman they called Fan Thompson, a real character, who used to smoke a clay pipe. She had a stall in front of the blacksmith's shop with another old character called Frizzer Jack. He looked after the hot mushy peas at a halfpenny a saucer full. He used the hopping plate as a table.

Ten-thirty would be the start with the big band striking up. The band would arrive about mid-morning Friday and marched from the York road to Wold End, its members all in their regalia. After a short break they would walk to Acklam for a church service then

return to Leavening for a slap-up hot lunch in the marquee, supplied by the landlord of the Hare and Hounds, Mr. King. As my mate and I were walking up the road Mr. King was coming down the road to the tent with a large plum pudding. We managed to get a sniff. It smelt great.

Saturday was the great day. There was cricket match. It got very exciting. At 6.30 in the evening it was sports for all, young or old. The oldest folk, who had gone past it, would stand by the winning line. And didn't they get excited when the women were racing! The old men would go hysterical.

As the evening drew on, that was when the fun would start. All the farm men and villagers from round about had come. The farm men were all dressed to kill with their bell-bottom trousers and their caps cocked up on three hairs.

When the pubs turned out it was great fun for young and old. The beer would soon start talking and it was all hell let loose. Who was fighting whom only the beer knew, and it was a case of "Get thee jacket off, weeal soon see who's the gaffer." Shirt sleeves rolled, spit on their hands, give them a rub; fists up all ready — then they would start arguing who was going to strike the first blow. A drop of blood and snot would fly, or someone would just roll on the ground. Most times it ended up with a handshake.

It just fizzled out. That would go on until midnight and everybody would go home happy, waiting for another year. It wasn't the same after the war. My mate and I used to get up early Sunday morning and go out looking for coppers. We never found any.

Burythorpe also used to have its own show, in a small marquee in the pub yard. They had engaged the local brass band to play for the dance in the evening. During the interval they were in the pub having a drink and had left their instruments on the table. One chap poured a pint bottle of stout into the bass instrument. In came the players feeling refreshed. "OK, lads, one, two, three..." Two big "oompahs" and up went the bubbles. All he said was, "Too good to waste" so I'll leave you to guess what he did with the contents...

****

It was a very damp Sunday evening in November, and I had only to go round the corner to the old pub, so for a joke I took some

22

blood-red powder and sprinkled it on the ground by the front door. It soon spread and looked like blood and showed up under the light.

The fun started. Out went a big, burly chap. He came rushing in shouting to the landlord "Ring the police, I've never seen so much blood in my life!" "B--- the police!" was his answer. It wasn't too long before there was bedlam and two chaps almost got to fighting. There were different opinions as to what could have happened — from a burst ulcer to a cut throat. Two brothers went out with a box of matches to have a look in the long grass at the back of the building. No hope.

Another went out and dipped his finger in the solution. He came back in: "That isn't blood, it's dried on my finger". He was told he wanted his head looking at for talking so daft and saying it wasn't blood. Morning came. Out went the manager to have a look. He had a shock, rang the police. Down came an inspector and sergeant. They took one look and concluded someone had done it for a joke.

Just imagine what the pub was like after this incident. We were playing darts in the room at the back and the marker shouted "Double 18" and the ceiling came down on top of us! We all looked as if we had been in a lime kiln. It was that low you could put your hand down the chimney and open the front door.

One regular was always boasting what he had done and what he could so. I was in the pub on Sunday night when he said he had six of the finest pigs at home that you could wish to see. One man said "I'll have a look at them when I go to market tomorrow". "If I catch you down my garden I will prosecute you for trespassing" declared the boastful one.

The pig dealer was jogging along next morning to market when he saw the fellow's wife standing at the front door. He pulled up and said he wanted to have a look at the pigs. "I'm the only b--- pig here!" she replied.

****

The days of knee breeches and leggings are a thing of the past but they do bring back memories to me. Many years ago there was a dance in the school at Leavening. There was no such thing as band in those days, just an old tinpot piano. I wasn't very old at the time, just a spectator. I can well remember two farm hands in their knee breeches and leggings. The funny part was, one was teaching his mate how to dance the Veleta. Not only was it a sight for sore eyes, the footwear really did match up with their dress; they were in what were known as beetle-crushers. What could you expect for sixpence?

The village dance used to be great fun in the late Twenties and early Thirties. It was very fashionable for the women to wear very long dance dresses which used to sweep the floor. Two chaps I knew very well went to a farm and got some horsehair. They cut it into very short lengths, went to the dance and sprinkled the bits on the floor. It wasn't long before the girls were all in the cloakroom, stripped off and having a good old scratch and the two jokers were having a peep through the windows enjoying it all immensely. What happened was that the horsehair pieces clung to the inside of the material and worked their way upwards.

A whist drive in the village hall was followed by a dance. The tea urn used to stand at one end. The MC called the interval dance and everyone got up except three chaps. Two kept the waiter talking while the other tipped about a pound of Epsom salts in the tea urn. By about 1.30 the place was getting deserted. The MC called for attention around 2 a.m. as the Vicar would like to say a few words. They were very short: "I would like to..." and off he went, not to return.

Chapter Three

"BRING HIM TO TEA SUNDAY"

Courting in those days was nothing like it is today. Courting today is all too easy, all the fun has gone out of it. They start school and no sooner are they courting, and by the time they leave they are thinking about getting married. It is nothing like it was in our schooldays. You would not see them running about the street at night then, Dad would see to that.

As they grew up, getting towards leaving school, and the dark nights approaching, the girls would make an excuse to go to church, and not without a sermon from the old man. As the night drew on he would have one eye on the clock, the other on the door, until suspense got the better of him. That meant he would march to the door...

"Is that you?" "Yes."

"Get in here quick. And who's the bloke? B--- off or I'll put me boot in quick."

He'd be off like a greyhound.

The main employment for girls in those days in the country was being a farm servant, hired on a yearly basis; long hours and poor pay. After a few years on the farm they would make for the town to live in as servants.

As the time went by and they were getting more mature, romance would start to blossom and the courting would become more romantic. Then the real problem would be breaking the news to her parents. Mother would be the first to know, so she could break the news to Dad; she herself had already gone through the predicament. After the good news had been delivered in most cases it would be Dad who agreed and in most cases it would be "Yes" and also "Bring him to tea Sunday".

In most cases, too, that could be a little nerve-wracking for the poor chap. Matters would soon be put right with a cup of tea and a bit of Mother's home baking.

In most cases it would end up with the pair getting married, and

25

that would be the day Dad would be looking forward to and a treat for the women to pass judgment on. The day came and the blushing bride appeared, with her father wearing his flat cap. Then the tongues would start in a style of their own, and this would be the conversation:
"She is, you know..."
"She can't be..." "She can't be..." "She can't be..."

****

Years ago weddings were nothing compared with today's standard, but nevertheless it was a marriage and that's what counted. No fancy dress or bouquet or taxi — these came later on — it was mainly shanks's pony, in other words: walk.

One couple who lived together unmarried had reached the age of seventy when he proposed to her, and soon they were married. He must have been feeling a bit amorous and soon found married life was not all married bliss. She threw a basin at him and he forgot to duck.

Another couple who were living together took a steady walk over to Acklam to tie the knot. The bridegroom didn't seem very interested in what was going on and when the vicar asked him for a ring he was too busy charging his pipe ready for a quick puff when he got outside. He had a surprise when they got outside — they didn't use confetti, no, it was pudding rice. Wasn't he happy!

Years ago weddings were a bit of a farce, and in this particular one the couple were both well matched, as they were both illiterate. When the Vicar read the marriage vow to the bridegroom and had finished, he (the bridegroom) just stood there and never opened his mouth, so they had a repeat. But there came no "I will"; he had an answer of his own, and this is what he said: "I might as well, that's what I've come here for."

Married life must have suited him. If he didn't say "I will", he didn't say "I can't" for he soon had a family of nine.

The first wedding I went to I was only 23. There were 20 of us who who went and everything had gone wrong. So I was asked to give the bride away. I had a little tuition before we set off for church. The first tragedy; half-way down the front garden path a whirlwind came over the top of the house and the bride's veil and dress caught in the pea-sticks. We had a right old game to disentangle the dress. So far so good. We got to the church and were met by the parson who asked if I was the bride.

After the service we all arrived back at the farmhouse ready for the spread — two thick slices of fat bacon and a drop of Yorkshire relish; no toast, no speeches. The band turned up — drums and a fiddle. You couldn't hear the drums for the fiddle.

We all arrived home safe and sound and very hungry after a most hilarious day.

****

When I was born, many years ago, many more, like myself, didn't know much about the facts of life. It was all very hush-hush and tight-lipped. It was like the secret service is today and one thing used to puzzle us: How could women get so fat and suddenly become thin again? If we asked any questions we didn't get an answer, just a dirty look.

We used to wonder what all the fuss was about, fetching the local midwife. It didn't mean a thing to us kids. The neighbours would be running in and out like scalded rats. By the time the Doctor arrived many times it was all over; all he had to do was to give the new-born a check-over just to make sure all bits and pieces were in order, and poor Mum had to stay in bed about ten to fourteen days. During that time we used to have a few visitors; first one would say he or she was just like Mother, some would say just like Dad.

It makes me think, sometimes, if we have got the right parents!

You had to see the perambulator (pram) to believe it. They had four large wheels and a canopy. You could have put a baby elephant in one. What a game it was to manoeuvre it about in such pig-sty houses; they make smaller cars today; you had to keep a good hold in them thar hills.

The most awesome thing in the house was the rocking cradle. It was made of wood and the rockers were approximately three foot long. I have wondered many times, we were lucky to be in one piece. My mother would go out occasionally at night for a chin-wag and the old man had an idea. The cradle was upstairs so he made a hole through the bedroom floor, tied a string to the cradle, passed it through the hole, sat in his armchair, cocked his feet up, got a book, and at the first sound it would "Rock-a-bye, Baby". It worked wonders. You can imagine what it was like, no axminsters in those days. His pal came in to see him one night; he thought the old man had gone potty.

Nevertheless, I was like a good many more. As I grew up I soon

27

learned that I wasn't born under a cabbage, or a prickly old gooseberry bush.

Five minutes pleasure
Nine months in pain
Two weeks in bed
Then at it again.

****

Whenever there was a bereavement in the village of Leavening, it used to be a sad day to mark the passing away of one of their men-folk. They were men of great character; there was only one thing on their minds — and that was work. They used to take a lot of pride in their work, nothing like today, and the wages were a mere pittance. Golden syrup was our main diet, wages 15 shillings a week.

When the day came for the departure of their beloved friend, it was always on a Sunday and the turnout was most impressive. To show their respect they would put on their best suit, such as it was. My father's suit was grey when bought. After 25 years it went green with old age; as neighbour said to my mother how smart he looked in his green suit, and she didn't make her any wiser.

When the day came for the departure, they came from near and far, and the only means of transport for the lad was the local horse and cart, so you just imagine what it was like for the poor old horse over the hills to Acklam, a little push required at times.

If by any chance you were an estate worker and the time came for the departure it was quite a unique occasion; the horseman who was in charge and his pals would arrive with a four-wheel dray and two large shire horses, and they always looked very smart and it would be a steady walk over the hills to Acklam.

I can well remember seeing the funeral of a pauper. He was a very old man, his name was George Lockwood and he used to live in Leavening. He was a strange character, like many more in those days. However, he finished his days down town in what was known as the Workhouse. When he died they conveyed his remains to Acklam with a pony and cart (no mourners). Just a short stay at Leavening crossroads to show a bit of respect. Words fail me to explain what the coffin was made of.

How's this for a pauper funeral, as usual pony and flat cart. The roads in those days were rather rough, something like the streets of

York with cobbles. As they approached, the coffin fell off, and this was his epitaph:

Rattle his bones, over the stones
He's only a pauper, whom nobody owns.

****

When I look back to my days as a kid at school it makes me wonder where some of the people of Leavening came from. They could have been an invasion from another planet, come down with a single fare and couldn't get back. But one thing was for sure, whoever it was, they were well educated where money was concerned. The trademark was well known in those days: short arms and long pockets, and they lived up to it. I often wondered why so many sported a beard, and then I realised that it could be beneficial in more ways than one: save washing and shaving and make a clean shirt last a fortnight. And really those were the days of spit and polish.

The working days for Mums and Dads were far from attractive. During the day the only bit of comfort was over the garden fence. A lot of women had never been inside a picture house. At the weekend you would see the upper crust making their way to the Chapel for a sing-song and sacrifice their donation for another week. And while this was going on quite a large number of the working men would assemble at the crossroads near the pub; no money for beer, they had to be content with a weekly ration of one ounce of twist tobacco.

There was another small group of five. Their meeting place was in the back lane. One old chap, his name was Smith, was one of two brothers and two sisters, who ran a thriving business. He would skin a fart for a halfpenny and use the skin for a cornplaster. Whatever conversation arose, he was always right; he was the chairman.

Just to prove how mean he was, he took me into his house one Saturday afternoon and there on the floor was his late brother in his clothes, even down to his socks. He tried to sell me his Long Johns for two shillings each. I wasn't that hard up.

There were no restrictions to shop hours, six to nine — a little later on Saturdays for reckoning up after a week on tick. A lad went in one Saturday and got a quarter of tea in my mother's name. When my mother went to pay her weekly bill she refused to pay for the tea. Old miserable told her he couldn't afford to lose fourpence. He

29

didn't get his money. He could always afford to smoke, it was hard to tell the colour of his beard.

One of the butchers was called Whitwell, very abrupt. Like many others I have gone at six o'clock in the morning with a bread tin for a penn'orth of liver — "Come back at eight and don't forget the money" — that was the one meal we used to enjoy...

There was an old man who used to live on his own. He used to sell fruit and kippers and collect rabbit skins. If it was first-class he'd give you a kipper, if not you had to be content with a small orange. His name was George Hall.

Jack Crofty was the man with two wooden peg legs fitted just above the knees, and he used the local pub. One night in the winter he went out to the toilet for a sit-down and his legs were sticking out level with the seat. Out comes a big burly chap straight into the toilet.

"Who's put the wheel-barrow in here?"

The chap must have been having a doze. He was dragged up the yard. When the culprit went back in the pub and was telling the landlord what he had done the alarm went up. "All hands on deck!" and out they went and there was poor old Crofty rubbing his head.

****

The most interesting thing of all was if you required the doctor. He came to the village twice a week. You had to leave a message at a certain house and that would cost you 2s.6d. (12½p in today's money). He would see you in the street for sixpence. My old dad waited for him one day and he was chewing a piece of twist tobacco. First thing the doctor said was "Open your mouth" and then remarked "I didn't know you ate it, I always thought it was for smoking."

These are some of the things we had to endure when we were kids. I have wondered many a times who concocted the things we had to take. They were all supposed to cure. Here they are: If you were a bit itchy, first thing in the morning two spoonfuls of brimstone and treacle. Another old wives' tale — it was good to take but, oh dear, it made us smell terrible. There was no comparison between that and sweet violets. It was more like midnight in the sewage works. The old school teacher didn't bother us much; a couple of sniffs and a rub of his nose and he was off.

If you had bad toothache, it was: Take a piece of brown paper, perforate it with a needle, dip it in vinegar, slap it on your face held on with a red handkerchief. You looked a real one.

Another old women's tale was: If you had a bit of chest trouble, get some goose fat and rub it well into your chest. It was always the same old story — "It's the finest thing in the world" — but you might as well have rubbed your chest with a brick.

Another brainy idea was: If you had a bit of frostbite in your feet, walk barefoot in the snow. I have often thought, I would have liked to have them out and rubbed their backsides in it. And what about this brainy idea? Whooping cough was another thing we had to endure. Another marvellous cure for this was to go to the blacksmith's shop and get a good whiff off the horse hoof when he was burning the shoe on to make it fit. It was cough, cough, cough. It was useless. When they passed on they took their patent ideas with them.

One chap was going bald and was getting worried, as he was quite young. So he asked his mate if he knew of a cure.

"Yes", he said, "go into a field and find a cowpat; but there is only one problem, you will have to keep your cap on for a month."

After two weeks of the treatment, he got a bit worried so he had a feel and he thought he was growing a tail. Rather worried, he went to see his pal. He soon had his mind put at rest. It was only a boil.

****

We had a tailor's in the village. The business was run by two brothers and in those days they were the best. The first long trousers they made for me were when I was 13. I shall ever remember, it was on a Saturday night and I had to stand with my legs slightly apart so he could take the inside length. He gave me a little touch and his remark was "Thu's got a bit of thi Uncle Thom in tha". Just to prove how good the material was, three of us got measured up for a blue serge suit. I saw one of them in 1946 and he was still wearing the £3.5s. suit and he said it was still good for a few years. He also remarked that he had never had to sew a button on.

It was no good trying to con the old tailor. If he saw you wearing anything he hadn't supplied he soon spotted. Next time the person went in to shop, just a short note: "Get clothes elsewhere." School clothes had to be bought in town. I was the one who had to wear my brother's cast-offs during my schooldays, so you can understand what they were like. Would you fancy sitting on a cold seat at school with the seat of your pants worn out and, to add insult to injury, wearing a very short shirt?

****

Two men were doing a bit of rabbit-catching in a hedgerow not far out of town. They put a ferret in the burrow and they struck lucky. One withdrew the ferret, put his arm down the burrow when along comes the local bobby. He gets off his bike and walks towards them. One chap was stretched out trying to extricate the rabbit, so the policeman tapped him on his backside. Thinking it was his mate, he said, "Stop it, you silly b—, I can just feel his b— arse,"

Remarked the policeman, "Yes, and I can feel your b— arse as well."

It was fun on a Sunday night in the winter when the pub turned out. They used to brew talking beer in those days: all talk, no fight. Sometimes you would see a bit of shirt, and that would be repeated a few times, then around twelve they would all go home until, another week, then there would be a repeat, and it would go on and on. It all seemed to finish when the war started in 1914. It was never the same old Leavening, they used to say — "happy and poor".

Chapter Four

NO SMELL OF SWEET VIOLETS

Many years ago the fatstock market was held on a Tuesday, then it was put back to Friday, in the days when there was no such thing as motor transport and all the cattle and sheep had to travel on foot. Pigs had it in style, they were carted in, so you can imagine what the roads were like. It was worse in the heat, they seemed to get very excited. After the sale a large percentage of them had to be driven to the station for despatch to towns in the West Riding. Still more smells, and it wasn't sweet violets — you had to see it to believe it.

This is what happened to a lad from the old village. His father took him down town to buy him an overcoat. After the purchase he told the lad to have a walk round the cattle market while he had a pint. He was walking between the pens and he got a bit too close when suddenly an old beast cocked up its tail and with one loud cough and before the lad had time to move, had plastered him from head to foot. And it wasn't the nice stuff women use. They used to say many years ago that the smell of farm manure gave you an appetite.

Saturday was a great day when the farmers' wives would invade the town with their produce such as butter, eggs, rabbits etc. and the next and most important job would be rushing round doing the weekly shopping, not forgetting their fish and chips, and then a walk round the open market. One thing used to amuse me and that was the number of chamber pots one chap sold. It was a case of buy now, try later, no guarantee. While all this was going on the old farmer would be in the cattle market. It was great fun watching them make a deal, they wouldn't budge. It would go on for some time and then very suddenly there would be a slap of each right hand.

Now the next problem was going back home. It would be around four; you had to see it to believe it. When it got to going-home time and the railway gates were closed — sometimes there was a slight hold-up at the station — what a trail-back of traffic. That's when the beer started to talk. There was a ranting and raving, more so if the

33

signalman showed his face on the top of the steps. He would shout, "Thu either comes fra Leavening or Acklam". And he wasn't far wrong!

****

Living in the country where I was born just after the turn of the century all we had for transport was the old horse or shank's pony, better known as walking, and that was the way the men knew it. The conveyance to town for women and children was known as the old covered cart, very high off the ground, fare sixpence return, children half. I went twice with my mother so I know what the journey was like.

The procedure of loading was rather difficult. The old cart was rather high and had only one step, and what made it worse was the dresses the old women wore. It was a case of up the old dress and a push from behind, showing their bloomers (better known as ham bags).

My schoolmate and myself used to stand at the other end of the cart watching the old women getting on and one accidentally lifted her skirt too high, not thinking what I could see!

Departure time was 9.30 a.m. six passengers and a journey time of about 90 minutes. It was like playing draughts; when you came to go downhill the old driver would shout, "Sit well back to keep the weight off the horse's back". When it was uphill it was, "Sit well forward to keep the weight off the horse's belly", in case the horse went off his feet. By the time they got to White Wall it was time for a little trot. The old women never stopped talking and later on in life it wasn't the birds and the bees. Just imagine having to endure that kind of trip in the winter.

On arrival the most important duty was the shopping. Before that the women had to count their money, and that didn't take long. Nevertheless, come to think, you could buy a roll of house paper for two pennies old money and make your paste with plain flour. Four o'clock and that was the end of the shopping spree and time for departure, with all their wordly goods and their bodies safely trussed into the cart. It was a long trek home, taking a little longer, with a few more "Sit back" and "Sit forward", and quite a few grunts and groans from the old horse.

And that was the way of life.

****

34

Living in a place like Leavening and other surrounding villages, it couldn't have been much worse at the North Pole. In those days bicycles were known as bone-shakers. They had no free-wheel, only a special step fitted to the outside of the rear hub. You had to jump on the bike from behind and with a bit of luck you would drop in the seat and catch the pedals as they were going round. If by any misfortune you misfired you could do yourself a slight injury, and it would bring a few tears to your eyes. There were no mudguards, you had to avoid water-holes. There was one brake and it operated on the front-wheel tyre.

The first car I remember seeing was a Ford. It would be around 1911, and was a novelty in those days. It was used as a taxi and brought the school doctor to visit Leavening School. There wasn't much shelter for the poor driver, it was the fresh air treatment. It was laughable when it came to a hill, but great fun when we had to give it a push. The next car on the scene was the doctor's. He used to drive an open top car winter and summertime. The only protection he had was the windscreen. He had a special coat for the winter; it was that long you could just see his feet. It must have done him good, he lived well into his nineties.

The first public conveyance in Leavening was an old lorry with solid tyres and was first used as a commercial transporter. It wasn't long before they had other ideas of using it as a public conveyance. A canopy was designed for special occasions, such as going to town or a trip to the seaside. There were only three faults with it: The dusty old roads, if you had false teeth keep your mouth shut, and last but not least for goodness' sake don't take any Epsom salts prior to the journey or you would soon be in trouble. I should know, I was the co-driver.

****

At the turn of the century Christmas Day was almost like any other. There was very little money about and times were very hard. The people that had a bit wouldn't part with much, there were a few old skinflints about. I, like some others, used to get up early Christmas morning and go round singing a little song and wishing them a Merry Christmas. You were lucky if you got anything. They would shout: "You are too late, it's six o'clock in the morning".

Later on in the morning you would hear other kids saying what Father Christmas had brought them. I would then go home and

35

ask my parents why he hadn't been to our house and this is the answer I got: "He got stuck in the chimney and they had to take him to hospital". What we had to endure when we were kids...

However, later on in the morning the carol singers would come round and then you started to get a smell of the dinner being cooked. Me and my mate used to have an extra sniff through the keyhole; it made us feel better; and as for presents we would be lucky if we got a secondhand Snakes and Ladders game.

Later on in life one thing I liked about Christmas was when we used to go carol singing; we would walk miles.

Now this is a story told to me: When five of them went carol singing round the farms and cottages on Christmas Eve, up in the hillside were four semi-detached cottages and one couple had killed a pig and they had been busy making sausages. These were in a bowl on the end of the table and they were all linked together.

The householder gave the carollers a drink and for goodwill they sang a carol inside. One chap shuffled round the bowl and started stuffing sausages into his pocket, not knowing they were linked together. When it came time to depart he was the last to go out, with about three feet of sausages hanging out of his pocket. It all ended up in good spirits, but the chap gave it a miss the next year.

To sum up, my idea of Christmas in the country could be very boring. It used to come and go, nothing ever seemed to change. It was a little better when you could go in the pub for a pint.

Now many years ago the local pub at Leavening used to make its own plum pudding a few months before Christmas and hang it in the bar. Once, when the landlord was out two chaps went in and kept his wife talking while another went into the bar and took the plum pud down and slipped some soap inside.

On Christmas Eve it was put in the pan on the hob of the old coal fire for the final boil. The old lady came in, took the lid off and bubbles galore went up the chimney. "It must be rich" she remarked. Then the moment of truth came. Lips smacked as out came the pud — and what an awful smell with it. The two chaps responsible had to go outside. They couldn't stand the suspense.

****

One Ebor Day my mate and I biked to Stamford Bridge and caught a bus to York. We had a nice day at the races and spent the evening in town. We intended to catch the 10 p.m. bus back to

Stamford Bridge but we parted company. So I had to wait for the last bus at ll p.m., got my bike and set off for home. I had gone about five miles when I saw what looked like a cow laid in the middle of the road. To my surprise it was my mate with his bike on top of him. I woke him up and he couldn't tell me what had happened. All he could say was that he was dreaming about me. We walked all the way home and it still remains a mystery what happened.

On another occasion we went down to the fair in Malton. We had a few drinks and then I left him; we agreed to meet for the last bus home. He was missing. However, just as we were to depart he made his appearance with hands, face and clothes all dirty. All I could get out of him was that he had gone to sleep and when he heard the fairground music he thought he was in Heaven. I found out afterwards that he had gone out the back way of the pub and had fallen into the coalhouse.

We got talking to a chap in the pub one Saturday night down town and he asked us what we did for a living. I said, rabbit catching. He paid for two pints and gave us 3s.6d. to send him a couple of rabbits on the 7 o'clock bus into town. We thought no more about it until the following Saturday night when he was there again. What a greeting we got! However, our friendship didn't last long and we never saw him again.

****

Now that spring is nearly with us once again, it does bring back a lot of memories to me. When I was at home in the country after a long dreary winter it used to be nice to see the old currant bun (the sun) coming up over the horizon, earlier as the days rolled by. It was nice to hear the chirping of birds hopping along the gutters of the houses. The cuckoo would be next. There was an old wives' tale that if you didn't make a wish when you heard the cuckoo you wouldn't have any luck.

Now the only wish I made was, let's have some nice sunny weather. What was nicer than to have a stroll in the field and then finish up with a lie down behind a bush among the buttercups and daisies and not a care in the world. That was, until an old cow came and had a peep, with her big beady eyes, then gently strolled away leaving me thinking that was the end. Oh, no, who else could it be, none other than the old gentleman himself, the old bull. Didn't he look pleasant, glaring with his big beady eyes, he must have thought it was one of his cow friends.

We waited a short while and when we saw our opportunity we made a hasty retreat.

To think what might have happened if he had come any sooner and caught us together, like a bacon butty sandwich. It would have been a bit of a scrat to get away.

It's nice to get the sun on your back now and again...

****

I have no doubt in my mind that a large majority of the Marwood family were Wesleyans. All our family, like a lot more, were the old Primitives, better known as the Ranters; not the snobbery type, we used to let rip more like the old Sally Army, with "Count Your Many Blessings", and "When Jesus Washed My Sins Away". One thing really got me guessing; they never had any toilets, and this is what happened one Sunday night in the summer...

When the time came for the preacher to deliver his sermon, it was "Come unto me all who are weary, worn and heavy laden, and I will give you rest". He only got to "laden" when he made a bolt for the door. He ran a short distance up the street, then across the road, over a garden fence, up behind the hedge and dropped his trousers, not realising that the people in the cottage at the top of the garden would see him — which they did. He must have been more laden than weary, for he tried to find a bit of grass. He was unlucky, by the way, he must have got hold of a nettle, the little dance he was doing.

****

This is what I was told by a person who lived in the bad old days, mainly before the turn of the century. He was a Leavening man. It was in wintertime and he was working away from home. On a Saturday after a booze-up he left to make his way home. He'd gone about two miles when a big burly chap walked out of the hedgerow and asked him if he had any money. He didn't hesitate; he put his hand in his pocket, grabbed his pipe and pushed it into the chap's stomach. The lad stood back and shouted, "I'll have you next week".

Monday morning he told his mate what had happened on the Saturday night so he lent him a revolver and the only two cartridges he had left. Saturday night came again. Same place, out walked the chap: "Have you got any money?" He whipped out the revolver, cocked it and fired it by the lad's ear! He said he jumped about two feet in the air and then took to his heels. He let the lad get a short distance away and then gave him the other bullet. Needless to say, he never saw him, again.

On another Saturday night the same person was coming home a different way. It was around midnight. He was about half a mile from the village when out walks this chap and all he had on was an old sack tied round the middle. The lad didn't speak, he just carried on walking along with him keeping his eyes open in case the other person got rough.

As they got near the first house in the village the lad said, "Are you frightened of me?" His answer was, "No fear". Then the stranger said, "Goodnight" and off he went.

The York to Malton road was another place the highwaymen used to hang out. In those days when a road could be a lonely place a farmer was making his way home on foot after being delayed in York. He had got about six miles from York when he was challenged by a rough-looking stranger demanding his money. The farmer said he could have it on condition that he put a bullet hole through each of his jacket sleeves so he could convince his wife that he had been robbed. He obliged. Then the farmer asked him to put one through his cap. "I've got no more bullets" he said. The farmer said, "I have" and gave him a good hiding.

My mother told me a story concerning a farmer who lived in the Wolds and he used to come down to Leavening to visit a friend. One night he had stayed longer than usual so his friend said he would go with him for the walk. They had got to the top of the hill when suddenly a big burly chap appeared from the hedge and set about the farmer. The chap got more than he had bargained for, but the farmer's mate was that frightened he took to his heels and made for home. On the way he lost one of his boots. He was too scared to stop to look for it and he arrived home minus one boot.

Meanwhile, the farmer went to a nearby farm and knocked them up. They went back to the scene with a gun and a lamp but couldn't find the culprit. All they could find was a lot of blood.

Chapter Five

TRAVELS ON A STEAMROLLER

The old York to Malton road was terrible; it was all twists and bends and very dangerous. It was all right in the days of horses and carts.

There were two railway crossings between York and Malton and Malton town was a real bottleneck. It was nothing to see traffic held up at Malton for a mile while the railway gate was closed there. A new road scheme was discussed many times, mainly with a bypass for Malton, but they used to say it would do away with trade from people passing through.

However, things got worse with more traffic on the road and it was getting out of control. And the dole queues got longer. Every week they decided to do something to improve the situation. The county council at Northallerton took the job on using local labour. There was every class of men you could think of — shopkeepers, butchers, bakers, farmers' sons — all glad of the money, although it was very poor pay.

It was just by chance that I got a job with an asphalt company. I was on a water scheme pipelaying near the railway yard and I had mentioned my interest to a foreman who at first said "No", but three days later asked me to start next morning, on condition that I was prepared to travel. That was to last 34 years!

It took me a week to get the hang of driving a steam roller, on the York-Malton road scheme. It was not just a case of rolling up and down, but of knowing how. The material was very hot and you had to roll it at the right time. The job had to be left perfect. It was the foreman's job first thing next morning to inspect the surface. I always made sure it was left as requested.

Not long after my work on the York-Malton road the steam roller was on its way out, to be replaced by diesel-powered machines. They were more economical, but didn't seem the same.

I once had the pleasure of visiting a private museum of steam engines and was given the chance to stand on one of the greatest show engines, the Winston Churchill. How I would have liked to have a run around on it — it was great!

My first experience with steam engines was with Binge Bros of Leavening. They had two threshing sets; a single-cylinder and a twin-cylinder Marshall compound. The latter was a very big engine, hills were no worry. I was the third man, with what was known as the band-cutter and the flag-man with no flag (that had been done away with). I used to help with the setting up and the oiling.

I soon took up my duties as second man and not long after took charge of the set-up. It was quite an experience. When I think of those days, I remember driving quite a few different steam engines. The last one was the smallest. I used to get blisters on my feet having to stand so near the firebox.

I got my job as a steam roller driver in June 1935. After eight weeks I was on the move. My first trip was to Doncaster. I left Monday morning at 7.30 a.m. and landed up in Sherburn-in-Elmet at 9.30 that night, at a top speed of two miles per hour. I got to Doncaster the next day at 9 p.m. The worst part of the journey was filling up with water but it was a lot of fun — and there were more travels and more fun to come!

After a month at Doncaster I left with my flagman on St. Leger Day. Everything was fine. We had no bother finding a place to stop and to have a meal and a pint!

Now the second day was a tragedy. I could only travel four miles on a tank of water and we were losing time having to go out of the way. About 12 o'clock we pulled up at a wayside pub intending to enjoy a pint. No drink. The place had been broken into and they had taken everything. The police were in at the time.

About two hours later we stopped a bread van and all he had was two small pork pies. We struggled on to a place called Everingham. Just outside there was a big house. I asked a lad outside if he knew of anywhere we could stay the night. He told us we were still three miles from the Hull road. We found a farmyard and the farmer said we could park up for the night and he would put us up.

It turned out that he had just sold up and he was off next morning. I asked him if he would make us a sandwich, which he did, and it looked lovely. But the bit of cheese was that hard and mouldy we couldn't eat it. The crust of bread must have been in the pantry for 12 months. We just had to go to bed hungry. The farmer

gave us permission to sleep in his barn on some new hay. We were soon asleep.

That left us with four miles to go the next morning. We hadn't gone far when we smelled frying bacon coming from a house. When we approached we were told to get out — the occupant thought we were gipsies. When I explained we were allowed to have a good wash and given a tasty snack. It was great!

When I reached the site I met my pals and we had a drink and soon after I was on my way to Leavening for the weekend. But my troubles were still not finished. I could only get a bus to within five miles. I had to walk it and that just made my journey worthwhile. I travelled many hundreds of miles in the next 12 years but those were the worst I had.

****

I had left my native Yorkshire for a two-week spell and I am still here (in the Midlands). On the 17th of April 1937 the foreman and myself set sail to a little town two miles from Leicester and it turned out to be quite an experience. They had found some lodgings which were far from home.

We had to walk to the work site on the Sunday morning. I had a shock when I saw the old steamer. It was the first I had seen where you got up on the back. It must have come out of the Ark. It was an Aveling Bartford with no gears and direct drive. The first weekend I did a few repairs and that helped a little. My mate went up home to Newcastle the second weekend and that was when the fun started in the lodgings. I arrived back at digs on the Sunday night after a night down town.

The old man was in his chair having a smoke. In comes the old battleaxe: "Where did you get to you old b----, left me to get back on my b---- own" she demanded. He said he had had to get back to let the lodger in. "B---- the b---- lodgers" she said. She sat down by me on the posh settee — just the bare wood, you had to be careful of the nails. "Have you given him his supper?"

"No, he didn't want any." It was on the table all right, a jar half full of vinegar with three onions in and a crust of bread, rock hard. In comes the son. He'd had enough. "Who's put that onion jar on the table?" He came to take it away. "Put that down, it's my supper" she said and broke a bit of the bread and put it in her mouth. It sounded like a jackass crunching snails.

43

The old man said he would go to bed and get ready for work in the morning. "Where are you going?" she asked. He said to Melton Mowbray to do some gardening. "Why, you lazy old b----, you are too b---- lazy to scratch yourself." That's life. And I was to see plenty of it in lodgings as I moved around with the job.

My mate and I were in lodgings at Newcastle-under-Lyme with some very friendly working-class people. The husband was telling us about his effort at making bread while his wife was ill in bed. She had threatened: "If you don't tell them, I will".

This is what had happened: he had put in 2oz of yeast instead of the usual 1oz. He put the mixture on the carpet by the fire to rise and went to do some shopping. When he came back the bread was all over the place. His wife shouted down: "Have you got the bread in the oven?" He couldn't keep it in the house, never mind the oven! He dug a hole in the back garden for it. When he got up next morning it had lifted the soil up like a little mountain.

Another time I was in lodgings it was my bath night and the landlady asked me to have it early. But she forgot to say there was a young woman staying with us. When I opened the bathroom door there she was in the bath! I did a quick retreat downstairs. The landlady was doubled up with laughter.

****

This is what an old cobbler in Oldbury thought about Yorkshire and its people. I took a pair of shoes to be repaired and he asked where I came from. When I said "Yorkshire" he said, "You want your b---- head looking at for coming to a b---- place like Oldbury." He shouted to his wife, "Come here, I've just told this chap he wants his b---- head looking at for coming here." She agreed with the old chap. He said they always went to Hull to see the married daughter. He didn't like the idea of coming away. The people were friendly and his wife agreed and said, "They always seemed more civilised in that part of England". I don't know where they went to. They pulled down all the houses. Most likely they finished up at Hull.

When I first came down to the Midlands I heard a saying: "He couldn't dance as good as Casey's ducks". This is what this chap used to do. He would build a small stage of thin steel place and put an oil lamp underneath to get the plate hot. Out would come the ducks onto the plate, and start hopping from one foot to the other.

The audience used to be amazed. They thought it was great. It went on for quite a while until the authorities caught up with him and that was the end of the dancing ducks.

Four of us went to lodge for a few days in Coventry with a young couple who weren't English. He did the waiting and would only talk to me. He came in one morning and whispered to me that he was going to bake some bread and wanted me to try it. Next morning, he came in with the bread loaf and said, "Feel it." I did and it was like a piece of concrete. That was the last I saw of it but when the bin men came and gave the bin a tug the bottom fell out of it. That was the end of the bread making. He said, "Call any time you are this way again" but we never did.

****

The men I worked with in one particular gang used to take a small quantity of tea each morning. One of the men thought the tea was rather weak at times. So one night just before they finished one picked up some dried horse dropping, wrapped it up and gave it to the teamaker. This man got up next morning, put on the kettle and put in the so-called tea. You can just imagine what it was like. He was fuming. When he got to work he called the man responsible everything but a Christian.

Playing jokes was a great hobby. At the firm I worked for later the plant foreman and chargehand used to have eggs and bacon for breakfast every morning. I was in the office taking a phone call and just for fun I took the pan off the shelf and scratched some marks in the fat, put the plate back on top and put the pan back on the shelf.

The following morning it was the chargehand's turn to fry. He took the plate off and said to the foreman, "The mice have been in the pan, I will give it a good clean out, it will be full of germs."

They sat down next morning to have their meal and the foreman said to Joe, "How could the mice get into the pan with the lid on?" Little Joe replied, "I know it's one of Fred's tricks". I saw Joe the next day and he said, "You and your b---- mice!" All I could say was that the pan got a good clean-out, it's what it wanted.

We were doing an asphalt job in the Humber works and this chap was standing a few yards away. I hadn't seen him before, I said, "Good morning, George', He replied, "Good morning, Frank. How's your wife Nellie and the children?" I had to think quick. "How's your wife and family?" I said. "Fine thanks". Before he left he said, "I'll tell the wife I've seen you and we'll have you over to tea one Sunday in the near future. Ta ta Frank" My mate was standing close and had heard the conversation. He said, "You are biggest old bluffer I've ever heard. I thought you were old pals!" I never saw the chap again.

I was in a pub in Cambridge one night and in comes this chap and sits down and we soon get talking: He asked me if I knew Birmingham and this is what he told me. He was in the 1914-18 War with this Brummie who told him that if he got through the war he could come to Birmingham to see him. He did so, but left it a bit late and couldn't find him and nobody knew where he had gone. As it was getting a bit late he made his way back to the town centre to find a place to sleep, as what money he had had been spent looking for his friend. He was told he was by the station and went along and found a building which was unlocked, so in he went. Just inside was a horsedrawn cab and he got in and went to sleep. It was just breaking dawn when he heard the doors open and as they got near the cab he looked up and asked, "What time is it?"

They didn't stop to tell him, he said it would have taken a greyhound to catch them. I told him it was a funeral parlour he had spent the night in. He said, "I didn't stop to look. I was faster than the police in the opposite direction and got out of town quick."

Before the war it was big business on a Monday morning, when money was scarce, to pop round to the pawn shop. This one chap used to take his alarm clock in for a half-a-crown every Monday morning and fetch it out Friday for two-and-ninepence. This went on for weeks. By then he'd had enough so he had an idea. Monday morning he took in a cod-fish head, all wrapped up. The pawnbroker took it and pushed it under the counter and gave him the half-crown without looking. He never saw the man again.

During the war we had a contract on an aerodrome and we had to make do with the labour they sent us. One chap was given the job as stoker on the bitumen tanks. Once he had clinkered out the fires and stoked them up again he would stand with his back to the tank, pull up his jacket, hands in pockets, then have a little shut-eye, forgetting the fire would soon burn up, and it did.

All at once he made a lovely dive. "Help me, I'm on fire!" His backside was a burning lovely. Everyone was helpless with laughter. He was still shouting for help. No luck. There was a tub of water. He went and sat in it: What a sight! Poor Johnny in his bare backside. It all helped to win the war!

At the depot we had one employee who was as thick as two short planks. He must have been educated at the tar works. His job was to sweep up and serve tea in the so-called canteen. The subject one day with the men was cremation and the tea-maker was trying to take it all in when the conversation finished. His comment was, "It must be an awful death to be cremated". Then he said, "Well, there's one thing, they don't feel much".

One chap went in one day with a bottle of pop and the tea-maker said, "I haven't got any, for sure." So the chap unpacks a few crates and finds three full bottles. "What's these doing here, then?"

"Oh" he said, "I'm keeping them for when I've got none".

They had been using an extra-long rope one day and had brought it back and thrown it on the floor of the shop. I told him to hang it back up in its usual place. When I looked in later he was standing there scratching his head. One of the chaps asked him what he was doing.

"I'm looking for the end of the rope but some silly b---- must have cut the end off." He didn't know where to start!

He was helping out in the blacksmith's shop for a short period, doing a bit of acetylene cutting. He was asked to cut a plate where marked. "Right" he said, "I'll cut it as straight as a duck's hind leg." That's something I would like to see, a duck with four legs.

TAILPIECE

On this note we take our leave of Fred, now firmly based in the Midlands as the 1939-45 war looms. Today, long since retired and living in a residential home, he enjoys listening to tales of the past from his elderly companions. Fred, who learned to type when he was 85, still hammers out long letters to me, full of his irrepressible humour. One of these he closed recently with the words: "Now, my dear friend, just one more thing. Keep your heart up, if your belly trails a mile".
Which sums it all up, Fred-style!

RADIO
radio

THE STORY OF
INDEPENDENT, LOCAL, COMMUNITY AND PIRATE
RADIO IN IRELAND
BY PETER MULRYAN

BORDER
line
PUBLICATIONS

FOREWORD BY DAVE FANNING